Flying with Chinese

KB Workbook

Shuhan C. Wang, Ph. D. • Carol Ann Dahlberg, Ph. D.
Chiachyi Chiu, M.A. • Marisa Fang, M.S. • Mei-Ju Hwang, Ed.D.

© 2007 Marshall Cavendish International (Singapore) Private Limited

Published by Marshall Cavendish Education
A member of Times Publishing Limited
Times Centre, 1 New Industrial Road, Singapore 536196
Customer Service Hotline: (65) 6411 0820
E-mail: fps@sg.marshallcavendish.com
Website: www.marshallcavendish.com/education/sg

Distributed in North America by:

CHENG & TSUI COMPANY
Bringing Asia to the World™

Cheng & Tsui Company,
25 West St, Boston, MA 02111
www.cheng-tsui.com
Toll Free 1-800-554-1963

First published 2007

All rights reserved. No part of this publication may be reproduced, stored in a retrieval system or transmitted, in any form or by any means, electronic, mechanical, photocopying, recording or otherwise, without the prior permission of the copyright owner.

ISBN 978-981-01-6676-2

Publisher: Lim Geok Leng
Editors: Yvonne Lee   Richard Soh   Rita Teng   Jo Chiu   Chong Liping
              Cao Zichen   Kuang Xiaoling
Chief Designer: Roy Foo

Printed by Utopia Press Pte Ltd

Preface

Flying with Chinese is a series designed to make the most of children's natural ability to learn language by creating meaningful contexts for learning and guiding them towards language proficiency, literacy development and cultural appreciation. Each book is based on a theme and integrated with other subject areas in the elementary school curriculum.

Flying with Chinese is standards-based and focuses on learners' performance. Some of the important elements in this series include the following:
1. Thematic planning and instruction, with emphasis on the principles and structure of a good story;
2. "Standards for Chinese Language Learning," which is part of the *Standards for Foreign Language Learning in the 21st Century*;
3. Principles of *Understanding by Design*;
4. Matching languages with children (*Languages and Children: Making the Match*).

Under three umbrella themes, each book in the series takes on a different but related sub-theme. These themes are interesting to the learners, connect with the curriculum of the elementary school, promote understanding of Chinese culture, and provide a context for language use.

The Student Book provides the basic story for the lessons, while the Workbook gives learners the opportunity to practice the language and use the concepts presented in the Student Book. The Teacher Guide suggests activities for each day and indicates when the Workbook pages are to be used.

Flying with Chinese focuses on a group of children who are learning Chinese together. These children and their families come from a wide range of backgrounds, and several are heritage Chinese speakers. One member of the group goes to China with her family, where she attends a Chinese school and shares her experiences with her former classmates. Throughout the series learners are introduced to legends, real and fictional characters of importance to Chinese culture, and significant customs, celebrations, and other elements of the Chinese way of life.

Flying with Chinese can be used independently or as part of a sequence of study in a program. Just as a child can fly a kite on his own or in a group, we hope that children will have fun flying these Chinese kites while gaining insight into the Chinese-speaking world.

我的朋友平平
My Friend Pingping

目录 Contents

Lesson 1	我和平平 Pingping and I	1
Lesson 2	平平有什么？What Does Pingping Have?	4
Lesson 3	春天来了 Here Comes Spring	7
Lesson 4	平平不见了！Pingping Is Missing!	10
Lesson 5	夏天来了 Here Comes Summer	13
Lesson 6	平平，你出来呀！ Pingping, Please Come Out to Play!	16
Lesson 7	秋天来了 Here Comes Fall	20
Lesson 8	平平在做什么呢？What Is Pingping Doing?	23
Lesson 9	冬天来了 Here Comes Winter	26
Lesson 10	下雪了 It's Snowing!	29
Lesson 11	我们大了一岁！ Pingping and I Are One Year Older!	32

 # 第1课　我和平平

✏️ 我

 我叫_____。
我的好朋友叫_____。

# 动物园

友

1	2	3	4
一	ナ	方	友

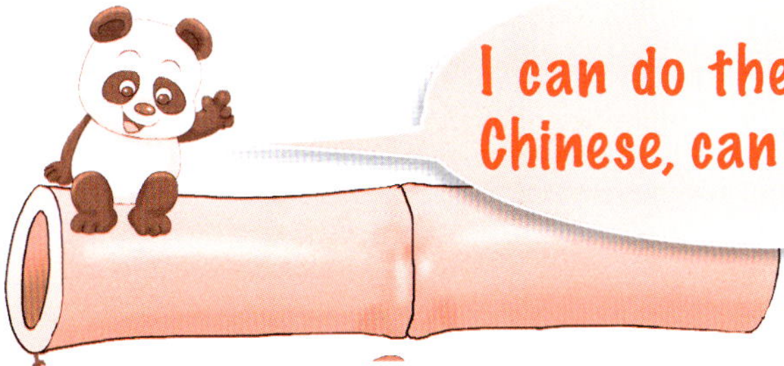

I can do these things in Chinese, can you?

I can...   Date   Date

❖ tell who I am and who my friend is (我是……)

❖ tell how old I am or my friend is (我五岁)

❖ identify a zoo

❖ recognize the *hanzi* "友", know what it means and how to say it

3

第2课　平平有什么？

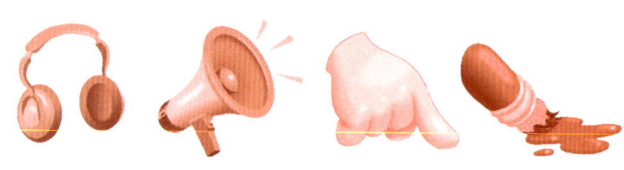 我有什么？

1. 眼睛

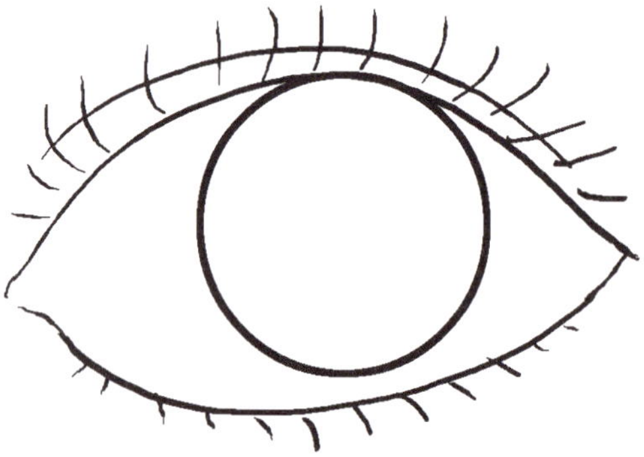

2. 耳朵

3. 鼻子

4. 嘴巴

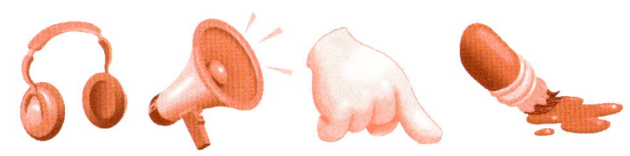

平平有什么？
你有什么？

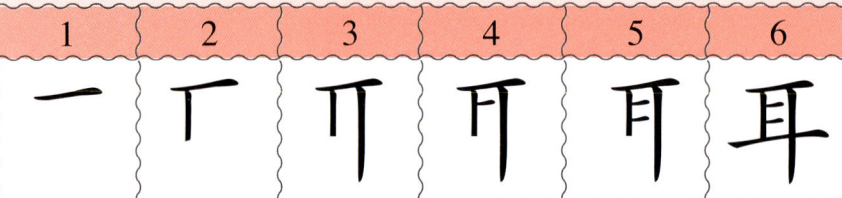

   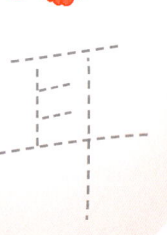  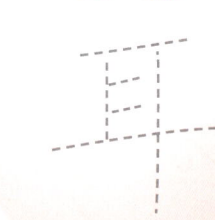

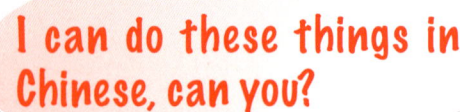

I can do these things in Chinese, can you?

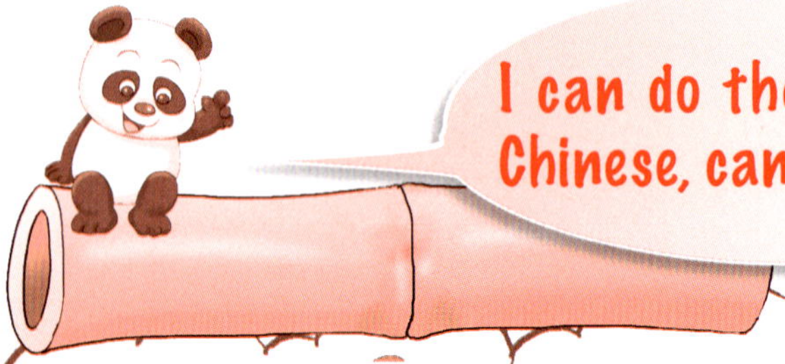

I can...	Date	Date
❖ name the parts of my, my friend's, or my pet's face		
❖ tell my friend that he or she is cute (可爱)		
❖ tell people what I have (我有……)		
❖ sing the song "我是大永" with the class		
❖ recognize the *hanzi* "耳", know what it means and how to say it		

第3课 春天来了

春天来了，常常下雨，天气不冷也不热。

1. 我能闻到什么？

2. 我能听到什么？

I can do these things in Chinese, can you?

I can...　　　　　　　　　　　　　　　Date　　Date

❖ talk about the weather in spring

❖ use my nose to smell (闻)

❖ use my ears to hear (听)

❖ recite the poem "春晓" with the class

❖ recognize the *hanzi* "雨", know what it means and how to say it

第4课 平平不见了!

 平平在哪里?

 平平不在_____,
平平在_____。

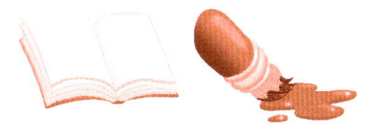

1. 平平喜欢春天。

2. 我也喜欢春天。

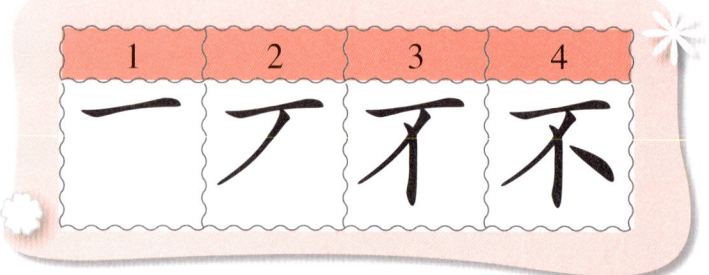

   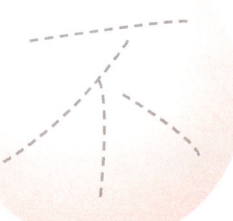  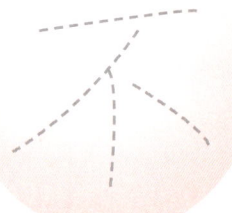

I can do these things in Chinese, can you?

I can...

I can...	Date	Date
❖ ask where my friends are (在哪里？)		
❖ tell "I'm here!" (在这里)		
❖ tell "I like..." (喜欢)		
❖ recognize the *hanzi* "不", know what it means and how to say it		

第5课 夏天来了

夏天来了,天气好热好热。

平平不喜欢什么？

1

2

3

4

 鸟

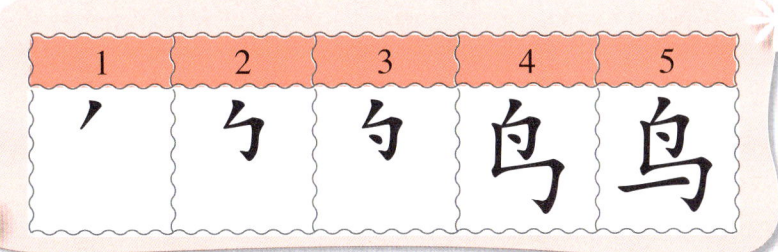

    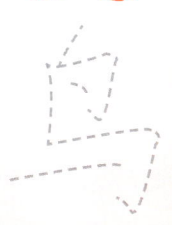 

 **I can do these things in Chinese, can you?**

I can...   Date   Date

❖ talk about the weather in summer

❖ tell someone how I feel about summer

❖ sing the song "妹妹背着洋娃娃" with the class

❖ recognize the *hanzi* "鸟", know what it means and how to say it

第6课 平平，你出来呀！

平平，你躲在哪里？
你出来呀！

平平在做什么？

1

2

3

4

  平平要吃什么？

 我要吃_____。

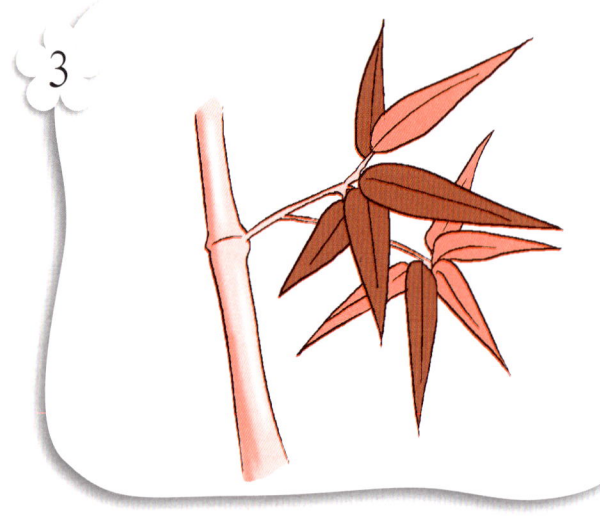

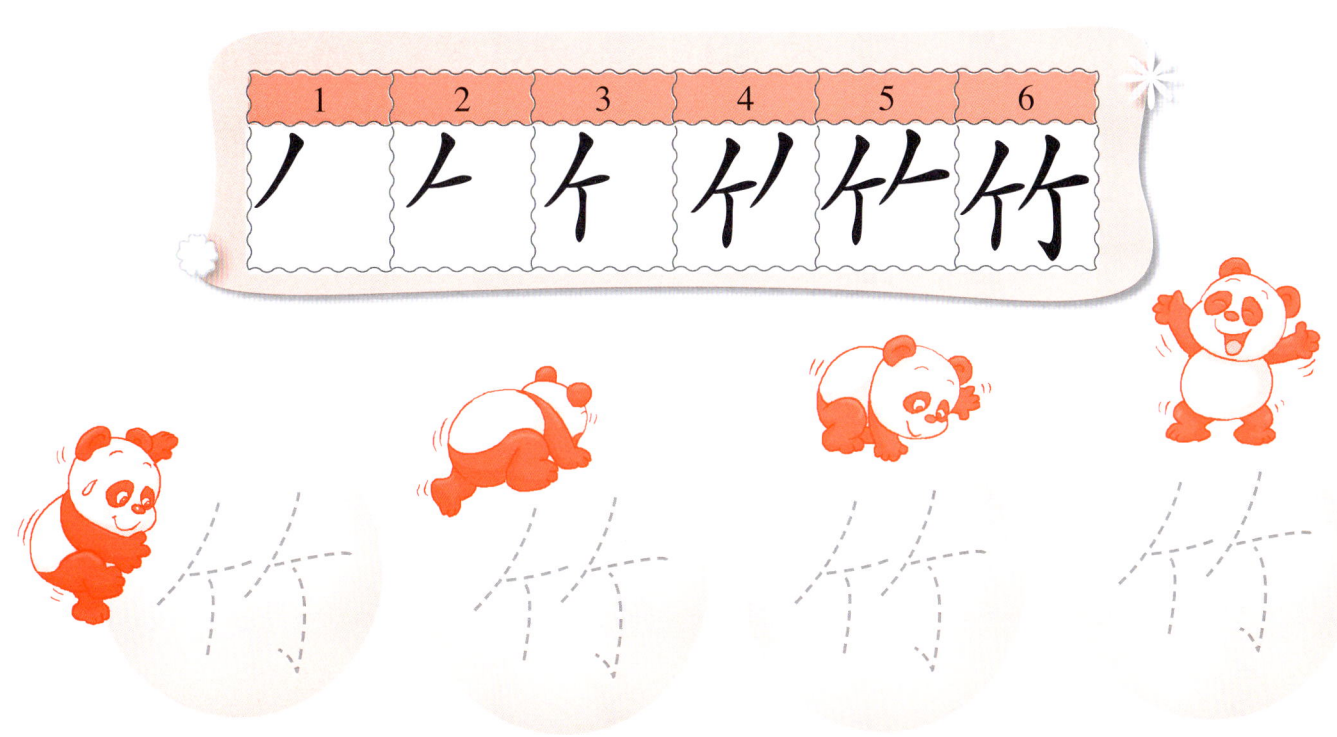

I can do these things in Chinese, can you?

I can...

❖ ask a friend to come out to play

❖ ask my friends if they are hungry

❖ tell I like to do something (blow bubbles, eat something, play with water, sing a song)

❖ recognize the *hanzi* "竹", know what it means and how to say it

Date   Date

19

第7课 秋天来了

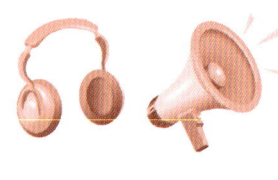

秋天来了,树叶有好多好多颜色。

红色

橙色

黄色

绿色

彩虹有什么颜色？

   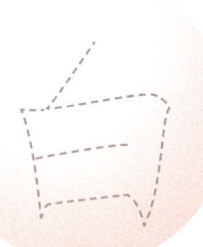

I can do these things in Chinese, can you?

I can...

❖ tell that fall arrives (秋天来了)

❖ name some colors of the sky, leaves, rainbow and a panda

❖ tell someone my favorite colors

❖ sing the song "彩虹歌" with the class

❖ recognize the hanzi "白", know what it means and how to say it

Date	Date

第8课 平平在做什么呢？

秋天来了，天气好凉好凉。

 平平在做什么？

1 吃苹果

2 玩落叶

I can do these things in Chinese, can you?

I can...   Date   Date

❖ tell someone about the weather in fall

❖ ask my friends to have fun with me, such
   as playing in the leaves, eating apples,
   playing with water, blowing bubbles, etc.
   (我们来……)

❖ recognize the *hanzi* "子", know what it
   means and how to say it

第9课 冬天来了

冬天来了，天气好冷好冷。

 冬天来了,平平和大永哪里错了?

I can do these things in Chinese, can you?

I can...   Date   Date

❖ talk about the weather in winter

❖ ask my friends if they are cold

❖ tell someone what I wear when I go outside to play

❖ tell someone how I feel about hot or cold weather

❖ recognize the hanzi "毛", know what it means and how to say it

第10课 下雪了

1 平平在滑雪

  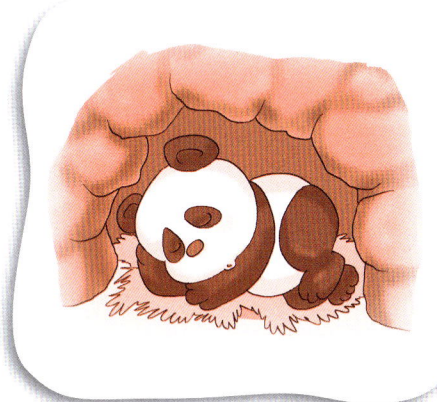

2 大永在堆雪人

  下雪了,平平喜欢做什么?

1

2

3

4

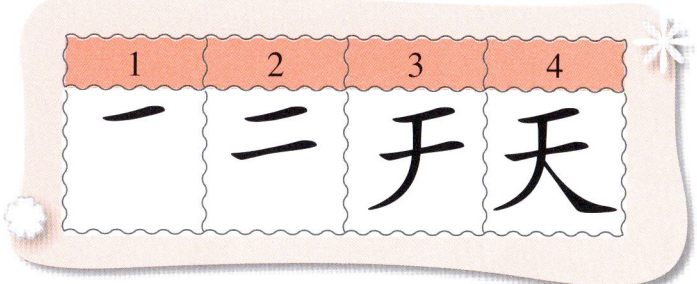

I can do these things in Chinese, can you?

I can...	Date	Date
❖ tell it is snowing		
❖ tell someone what I like to do in the snow		
❖ say the rhyme "大熊猫" with the class		
❖ recognize the *hanzi* "天", know what it means and how to say it		

第11课 我们大了一岁！

1. 春天到，放风筝 ● ●

2. 夏天到，去游泳 ● ●

3. 秋天到，采苹果 ● ●

4. 冬天到，堆雪人 ● ●

   大一岁！

1

去年的照片

今年的照片

友 天 雨 鸟 子

毛 不 竹 耳 白

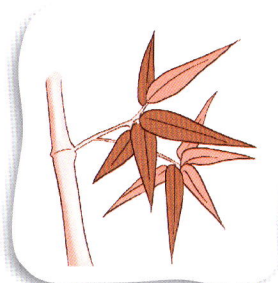 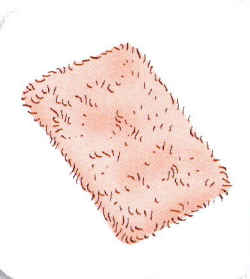  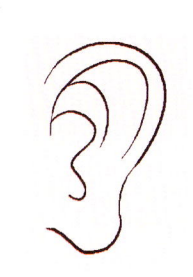 

春夏秋冬过一年，
你和我又大一岁。

I can do these things in Chinese, can you?

I can...

- tell that I'm one year older
- tell the four seasons of a year
- tell at least two parts of my face and what they can do
- say the rhyme "大一岁" with the class
- recognize the 10 *hanzi* that I learned in this book, know what they mean and how to say them

Date   Date